And the Beagles and the Bunnies Shall Lie Down Together

"HOW LONG, O LORD?"

And the Beagles and the Bunnies Shall Lie Down Together

The Theology in PEANUTS

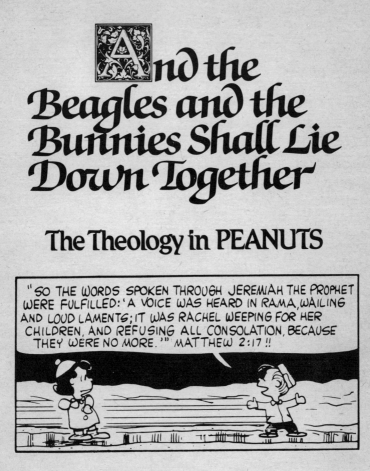

"SO THE WORDS SPOKEN THROUGH JEREMIAH THE PROPHET WERE FULFILLED: 'A VOICE WAS HEARD IN RAMA, WAILING AND LOUD LAMENTS; IT WAS RACHEL WEEPING FOR HER CHILDREN, AND REFUSING ALL CONSOLATION, BECAUSE THEY WERE NO MORE.'" MATTHEW 2:17!!

Charles M. Schulz

An Owl Book

Holt, Rinehart and Winston / New York

Published by Holt, Rinehart and Winston,
383 Madison Avenue, New York, New York 10017.

Published simultaneously in Canada by Holt, Rinehart and
Winston of Canada, Limited.

Library of Congress Catalog Card Number: 83-83150

ISBN 0-03-071083-9

Printed in the United States of America

10 9 8 7 6 5 4 3

ISBN 0-03-071083-9

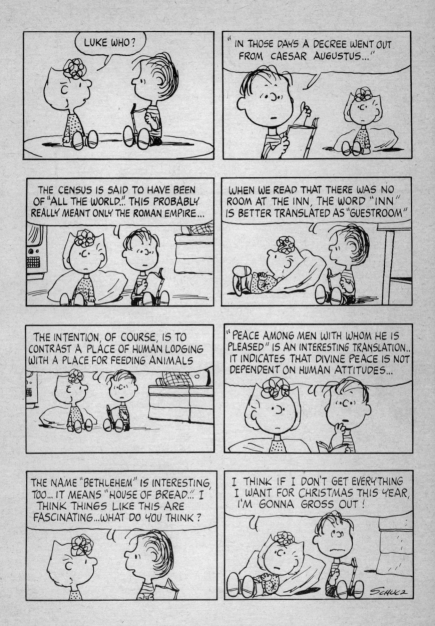

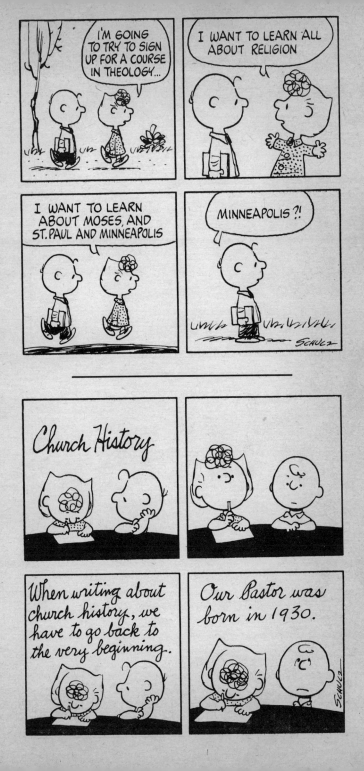

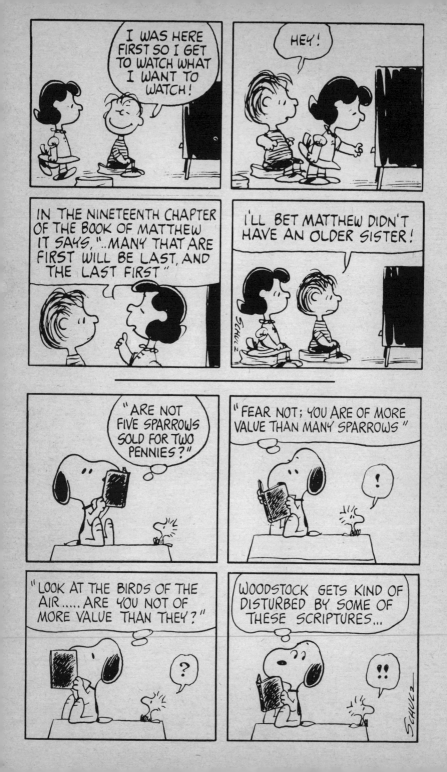